PTA DAD

Foul-Mouthed Poetry & Prose from a Real-Life PTA Dad

By Tomás Romero

MOONBEAST MEDIA

MOONBEAST MEDIA

Moonbeast Media, December 2020

ISBN: 978-1-7361949-1-1 (ebook)
ISBN: 978-1-7361949-0-4 (print)

Formatting by Polgarus Studio
www.polgarusstudio.com

Cover design/layout by Rachel Kerns

Copy edited by Toni Perling

Author photo by Ryan Romero
www.ryanromerovideo.com

Author Website
www.tomasnromero.wordpress.com

Printed in the United States of America

For Bean & Biscuit, my two favorite B's

CONTENTS

Introduction 1

Goldfish 5

She Only Comes Here For The Snacks..........................6

Miss America..7

Advanced Maternal Age..8

Deena Chen Don't Fuck Around 10

The Dudes Who Dad 11

That's Not Coffee In Her Tumbler 13

The Bruised Heart Of Mia S. 14

Lyft Mom...15

Parliamentarian Pam 16

Pajama Dad 18

Secret Smoker Sandi 20

McBullshit..21

Kandy With A K 22

Electrolit...24

The Irish Rose 25

Do Or Do Not..26

Kiki Mendoza..27

Play Date..28

Day Drinking 29

In Defense Of Karens 30

Seven Sofias 31

Lululemonati 32

Measure QX..33

Galarama 35

Regime Change 37

Principal P. 38

Vihni, Vidi, Vici 39

The Keymaster 41

The Poetry Of Postmates 42

Stay Up Late 43

Happy/S.A.H.D. 44

Ariana Grande 45

Crisis Queens 46

Frenemies 47

Daddy Manbun 48

Almond Paste Alma 49

Heather RBF 50

Punk Rock Mom + Sister Mom Jeans 51

The Kingmakers 52

Checked Out 54

#Voluntold 55

Tammy Talks Too Loud 56

Nobody Looks Pretty On Zoom (aka May 2020) 57

Working Moms 58

La Reina de la PTA (The Queen of the PTA) 59

PTA Confidential 61

About The Author 63

INTRODUCTION

Believe it or not, I have only fallen asleep at a PTA meeting once. It was on Zoom and I was muted, so, I'm not sure that really counts. I mean, hell, half of the parents at our last virtual meeting didn't even have their cameras on, so they might have been sleeping too.

Either way, I get it. PTA meetings can be a slog and volunteering is hard. Especially for the uninitiated.

Speaking of, if you have no idea what a PTA is, I get that too. The PTA, or Parent Teacher Association, is a formal organization – we actually have legit membership cards and t-shirts and shit – of parents and teachers who raise money and help "facilitate parental participation" at our kids' school. On the national level we also advocate on behalf of school-age kids everywhere.

In other words, we fight the good fight. Mostly.

And while I've never held an official PTA board position, I've had a fairly stellar attendance record over the years at our meetings and I definitely volunteer and show up for shit. Even if it's raining. Hell, especially if it's raining!

And though I might bitch about rounding up donated coffee and day-old bagels for Breakfast with Buddies or manning the volunteer sign-in table at the Boo Bash, the truth is, I live for this shit. Really.

I never would have expected it when I was younger, but volunteering seems to kinda be my jam as a parent. And if I can teach my daughter one lesson before I die it's that volunteerism and giving back to our schools and communities is as American as apple pie and Oprah.

But like our ever-evolving country, even the best-run PTAs are often well-intentioned works in progress. Flawed, fluid, messy and argumentative AF. And that goes double for the badass parent volunteers who run them.

Which is exactly what makes them so much fun to "wax poetic" about.

Happy reading!
TR

PS: The people and situations depicted here are fictitious. Any similarities to actual PTA parents, living or dead, are purely coincidental.

Except for that one mom. She knows what she did.

THE POEMS

GOLDFISH

Crafty, smart, and brimming with passion
was PTA president, Jenny McCashin

A whiz at fund raising and hot glue gun gluing
it was her penchant for goldfish that became her undoing

Jenny suggested live goldfish as prizes
at the Winter Fair booth everybody despises

"Goldfish are classics, we need them this year!"
cried Jenny McCashin as her board members cheered

But goldfish as prizes were never a fit
for a school with a garden and parents who are lit

So the woke, crunchy parents voted her down
and Jenny McCashin promptly left town

And now the only goldfish you'll find at our fair
are dusted with cheddar and puffed up with air

SHE ONLY COMES HERE FOR THE SNACKS

Her kids don't even go here
she comes here for the snacks

Cookies, fruit and donut slices
paired with coffee she takes black

She sits back near the bookcase
in the cheap seats by the door

And slips away before we vote
or count her for our quorum

But the jokes on you, freeloader
because the snacks are only great

At those first few meetings in the fall
before the winter break

MISS AMERICA

Miss America cried
every night at our meetings
Sharing meaningful quotes
with lots of super deep feelings

But she was much less effective
at getting shit done
And won re-election
by a vote margin of one

And though her gavel was tainted
by that nasty election
She forged bravely onward
in the face of rejection

And finished term two
with her usual flair
Spouting wicked good pull quotes
from Oprah and Cher

ADVANCED MATERNAL AGE

Betty, Jane, and Kiki
were the oldest moms at school
And when their kids hit third grade
they thought it might be cool

To start a band together
called Advanced Maternal Age
And jam about their struggles
out loud upon a stage

Punk hooks and catchy lyrics
were totally their thing
And luckily, for all involved,
those MILFs could really sing

They sang about their issues
conceiving healthy kids
With jams about lame doctors,
miscarriages, and SIDS

They never cut an album
but shredded nonetheless
For the few short years they graced us
with their grungy effervesce

Critics called them geriatric
and sometimes "L.A. old,"
but anyone who saw them play
heard those mommies spinning gold

And though Betty, Jane, and Kiki
broke up by seventh grade
The legend of their badassery
is kinda tailor made

For a poem about three valley moms
who refused to be waylaid

DEENA CHEN DON'T FUCK AROUND

Deena Chen with the perfect hair
was always keen to host or chair

Her house was epic and so was her wine
and we always had a fabulous time

But Deena Chen don't fuck around

When that lady says an impromptu
play date/board meeting/wine-and-cheese-soaked box top
cutting party
ends at 10:00PM

You best be rinsing your glass in the sink
and ready to go by 9:45

At.
The.
Latest.

Deena Chen has shit to do and she will see you at drop-off
So, thanks for the laughs and get the fuck out

Seriously, it's 10:05

THE DUDES WHO DAD

Marty built our Buddy Bench
in his backyard with a drill

Greg designed the Dino maze
which he built with Des and Phil

Ara brought the baklava
and ironed out our books

And Tarek didn't show up much
but man, that dude could cook!

Jack co-ran the science fair
and Greg always stayed late

To clean shit up after events
and lock up the main gate

Rick secured our taco truck
Rocker Dad DJ-ed our dance

And I showed up to a meeting once
in real shoes and pants!

PTA Dads may still be rare
in other towns and schools

But our volunteer jam is dead on-point,
DILF-tactic and cool

The ladies outwork us by far
I know that for a fact

But my hat's off to the dudes who dad
who get involved and act

THAT'S NOT COFFEE IN HER TUMBLER

That's not coffee in her tumbler
or water in her flask

And that smell is not skunk
if you really must ask

But she keeps her shit together
the best way she knows how

And her kids are smart as fuck and in GATE
So…how you like her now?

THE BRUISED HEART OF MIA S.

Lips like pretty pluots
eyes dark almond brown

Slinky Mia S.
was the meanest mom in town

She'd married advantageously
to start her life off right

With a rich old Euro bastard
who she even kind of liked

But when her husband left her
Mia wilted on the vine

And channeled her frustrations
into fundraising and wine

Her daughter took it hard
and went goth by second grade

And now moody, casual cruelty
is mini Mia's stock in trade

Mia's not much better
but she raises loads of cash

So we put up with her shit
and when she leaves, start talking trash

LYFT MOM

Single mom Suzy drives
for Uber and Lyft
Drops off the kids
and logs in for her shift

Stashing the car seats
in the trunk is a must
As is vacuuming up
all the graham cracker dust

And though her car still smells
like kids and old dog
Her in-cabin treats
leave her riders agog

Juice boxes and gummies,
Lunchables with ham
All complimentary, of course,
because that's just Suzy's jam

She wraps up by 2:00
for pick-up at school
So tip her well, shitheads
please try to be cool

PARLIAMENTARIAN PAM

Slim Jims for dinner
pot pies for lunch
Anything brown was
good in a crunch

Her kids didn't listen
her friends didn't care
Her day job was boring
she hated her hair

But one night a month
Parliamentarian Pam shined
At our PTA meetings
where she controlled time

Pam couldn't police
what we'd do, think or say
But if you went over on time
Pam would not let you play

One night a month,
Pam was in charge
One night a month,
Pam was power writ large

She managed the time
sewing order from chaos
With the clock on her phone
which Pam ruled like a bytch boss

And it was...glorious!

PAJAMA DAD

Every school has that dad
every town has that guy
That makes it look easy
without batting an eye

He's handsome and charming
and makes lots of money
And tells jokes that are clever
and actually funny

Pajama Dad is not that guy

With scruffy metal band hair
he always looks kinda baked
In his robe and pajamas
with his yard left unraked

But PJ Dad loves his kid
so he walks him each day
Hand in hand across the street
to that shiny school gate

But when it comes to timeliness
PJ Dad is worse than me
And when I see him in the morning
I know that tardy we will be

So I kick my kid out of the car
and tell her to run like hell
"Pajama Dad is beating us!
Run! I hear the bell!"

SECRET SMOKER SANDI

Everybody knows she does it
her clothing smells the tale
But Sandi's secret smoking
happens behind a veil

A sunny sheen of wellness
she presents each day at school
Where yoga pants, Pilates
and kale smoothies are the rule

But poor, sweet Sandi's secret shame
is smoking in her car
And I'm not talking primo weed
but chemicals and tar

I wish that I could help her quit
or tell her that I know
But that would never really fly
as Sandi's all about the show

McBULLSHIT

I don't like to fat shame
because I'm fat as fuck myself

But lying about fast-food love
is just lying to yourself

So when mean Milady McRib
with the fattest kids at school

Says she raised her cherubs
with one simple, guiding rule

Never to eat McDonald's
not ever, even once!

But Happy Meal toys aplenty
lay scattered in her trunk

Someone is clearly lying
and I call serious McBullshit on that

KANDY WITH A K

Kandy with a K
has a colorful way
Of discussing her food allergies

Every.
Damn.
Day.

She can't tolerate lactose
or eggs and bulgur wheat
And don't even get her started
on chicken and meat

She's a lifelong pescatarian
if you really must know
And that's just act one
of Kandy's first show

The menu is her script
the table her stage
So when lunching with Kandy
please do not engage

In even casual convos
about gluten, soy and dairy
Or that time she got so sick
from that single, red strawberry

Keep your chats simple,
glossy and stupid
Instagram, Twitter,
Facebook, OK Cupid

And whatever do you,
even if she asks
NEVER put that chick
in charge of our snacks

ELECTROLIT

Super toned and hella fit
Claire's dad is Electrolit

He jogs to school and then back home
he even jogs while on the phone!

He's kinda hot and super clean
and has a wife who's crazy mean

He played that frat dude on that show
and still maintains his youthful glow

The moms all love him, the dads do too
he's even friends with you-know-who

I'd love to knock him or wish him ill
but he's just too damn electro chill

I think maybe he's a robot

THE IRISH ROSE

The Irish Rose moved here
from Pittsburg, PA
To host the news and the weather
on good old KTLA

That's all over now
and today she has a website
Posting yogatastic videos
and crunchy tips on how to eat right

A fixture of our PTA
with long, flaming red hair
She chairs our Spring Fling and our room reps
with a regal, runway air

Careful to surround herself
with weeds and dull, grey cat grass
The Irish Rose shines brightest
among the weirdos and the outcasts

Petty, paranoid and vengeful
she has few real friends
But stands tall in our garden
with thorny stems that never end

DO OR DO NOT

You don't have to be
as totally OCD
As Heather RBF
or that new mom, Katie P.

But if it's three-o-clock
on the day of the Boo Bash
And you don't have prizes,
balloons or petty cash

You are seriously fucked
and so is our booth
So, I'm going full-on Yoda
to tell you the truth

There is no try
in our PTA
Do or do not
or get out of the way

KIKI MENDOZA

Most parents have a limit,
two events per day
But Kiki's calendar is brimming
and she loves it that way

Two bounce house bday parties
and a BBQ with friends
Were not exceptions but the norm
on most of her weekends

She volunteers for PTA
and in the classroom too
She also leads a Girl Scout Troop
and Sunday School to boot

Her kids and husband love the chaos
onboard her crazy train
Where Kiki leads, adventure follows,
even in the rain!

And though she's always game
for some wine, Netflix and chill
Kiki's toughest daily challenge
is simply sitting still

PLAY DATE

I don't have to like you
to let my kid play with yours
But it definitely helps

Alcohol helps too

DAY DRINKING

Red cups at Verdugo
coolers full of wine
Fancy White Claw cans
will do me just fine

If the stoners from Burroughs
can light up nearby
I see no good reason
why we can't imbibe

We'll Uber if we have to
and walk home with the kids
So top off my mom juice
Kiki even brought lids!

IN DEFENSE OF KARENS

I know it's kind of chic right now
to call mean ladies Karen

But all the Karens I know
are chill AF and caring

Some of them might look the part
but deep down they're hella cool

So, when you see them selling shit for us
each day out front of school

Don't make jokes about their names
or make them feel nervous

Buy a membership,
keychain, logo hoodie, mixed bag,
or whatever other branded tomfuckery
that lady is selling,
in the rain,
to raise money for your school

And thank her for her service

SEVEN SOFIAS

There were seven moms named Sofia
in our fifth grade class
Which made telling them apart
a royal pain in the ass

I'm not knocking the name
because it's really quite pretty
But Sofia's four and six
were sometimes kind of shitty

It's not their fault, of course,
I mostly blame their parents
But if given the choice
I'd rather hang with the Karens

LULULEMONATI

Regina George in Nulu
Heather Chandler at forty
All blonde hair and long legs,
so incredibly sporty

Forever walking and talking
and power piloxing
Cleansing and fasting and
beetroot detoxing

Know them by the logo
writ large upon their pants
blended with seaweed
imported from France

They know everyone
and they see everything
So keep an eye out, Old Navy,
or they'll eat you by spring

Most of them mean well
some are just mean
The key is discovering
the difference between

MEASURE QX

Super Liberal Lexie
pushed it hard as hell
but good old Measure QX
was not an easy sell

Hoping to secure funding
for art and music in our schools
and intervention specialists
to give kids coping tools

QX was a stop gap
to keep those things afloat
But the old-guard libertarians
really rocked the vote

And shot Measure QX down
not just once, but twice!
To spare themselves a tax increase
that they just didn't like

"We want Sacramento
to fix this shit instead!"
They screamed from their lawns
while our school system bled

Down but not out,
Lexie vowed to keep on trying
While she prayed for the day
those old bastards start dying

GALARAMA

Despite a guest list
that was less than elastic
Our first PTA gala
was straight-up galatastic

Pretty, shiny,
oh so Instagrammable
The dress code said formal
so Lexie wore something flammable

But glitz comes with a price tag
have-nots need not apply
The bar was no host
and the ticket price high

Teachers got a price break
or so she was told
But the whole gala concept
left Lexie quite cold

"This is Burbank not Brentwood,"
Lexie huffed as she bid
On overpriced Marvel swag for
her husband and kid

So she skipped the next gala
with its sky-high overhead
And planned an old-school
bake sale fundraiser instead

REGIME CHANGE

Pies in the face
are fun for a while
As is a new leader
with grace, wit and style

But she should have come
with a warning label
About what to expect when
things get unstable

Use at your own risk
keep away from your eyes
This one will burn you
and might even lie

She didn't come with a label
so many bridges were burned
And when school started up
she just never returned

PRINCIPAL P.

Principal P.
was cooler than Pi
The kids loved his jokes
and for a time, so did I

But when Principal P.
made Maddie's mom cry
For daring to question
or even ask why
Our camp fund raising efforts
were running awry

We started to wonder
before we could aye
If Principal P.
was still our kind of guy

He had made a mistake,
of that I am certain
By letting us see
behind his snark curtain

And Principal P.
who once ruled over us all
Was out of a job
by the following fall

VIHNI, VIDI, VICI

She came from Orange County
by way of Calcutta
With a pork Vindaloo
that was better than buttah

But Vihni didn't come here
to raise kids and cook
So she set out to do
whatever it took

To make herself useful,
friendly and kind
At our PTA meetings
by speaking her mind

And though her husband, Aadip
never quite understood
Vihni's drive to help out,
volunteer and do good

He didn't dare try
to keep her away
From her newfound side gig
at our school's PTA

Vihni's secret weapons
were IT and math
And planning and recruiting
upon our behalf

So she rallied the other
young Indian moms
And changed the face of our board
from bright white to bronze

THE KEYMASTER

The Keymaster knows
where everything's kept
And under which rug
all our secrets are swept

She runs a tight ship
and a tighter school shed
That she keeps organized
with a list in her head

Cash boxes and banners
games and Square readers
She'll even score you some cables
from the back of the theater

But the Keymaster lives
by two simple rules
Don't waste her time
and don't fuck up her tools

If you can abide
then you're good as gold
And she might even spill
some of the tea she's been told

If you're lucky...

THE POETRY OF POSTMATES

When his family goes to bed
Papa Postmates gets busy
Delivering fast food to stoners
all over the city

He's seen homeless hotels
with couches and drapes
And strange folks on scooters
with great flowing capes

He's seen coyotes and possums
and large families of skunks
And Thai Town trans hookers
who were totally punk

Vampires on Sunset
and ghosts in the hills
Sometimes the tips
even cover the bills

But the best part of Postmating
is the freedom to write
In the front seat of his car
in the dead of the night

STAY UP LATE

Whoever made up that shit about going
to bed early and waking up healthy and wise
Has never stayed up all night gaming with their kid

That shit is magical!

HAPPY/S.A.H.D.

Stay-at-home-dad
rhymes with sad
There's a reason for that

It ain't all sunshine and rainbows

Except for those days,
you know,
when it kinda is

ARIANA GRANDE

I secretly like Ariana Grande's music
Like, a lot
Don't tell my kid

CRISIS QUEENS

Brooke and Candy M. were
best friends since ETK
Attached at the heart and hip
they loved their PTA

Quick to volunteer
but less quick to help out
They've pulled the "working mom" card
more times than I can count

Traffic and sick kids worked too
when making their excuses
I wouldn't call them assholes
but they're really kind of useless

So if they say they'll help you
you'd be wise to triple book
Because crisis comes in duplicate
with Candy M. and Brooke

FRENEMIES

Keep your friends close and your frenemies closer,
said President Poppy on her way out the door

That mom who burned you in Pre-K
might just come back for more
Or, she might totally save your ass in middle school

Pace yourself accordingly

DADDY MANBUN

Daddy Manbun wasn't hot
but he had killer hair
And carried himself
with a chill, hipster air

He liked yoga and meditation,
reading and art
And helping out at the school
and the local skate park

Charming and funny
he had a super cool son
But hid a hard right agenda
beneath his manbun

And while that in itself
isn't always all bad
Trump love just didn't jive
with his rep as cool dad

And when his true nature emerged
in fiery posts online
Daddy Manbun was unfriended en masse
which suited me just fine

ALMOND PASTE ALMA

Almond paste Alma was always
trying new shit
Hipster takes on old favorites,
man, that gal would not quit

Her black bean lasagna
and tamales were great
but try as she might,
Alma just could not bake

Substitutions might work
with her savory snacks
But her almond paste cupcakes
made us all want to yack

Flavorless and hard,
Alma's cupcakes looked dead
Next time I hope she brings
store bought instead

HEATHER RBF

I don't like the term because
it's sexist as all fuck

But Heather wore it as a badge of honor
like a logo on her truck

And Heather's resting bytch face
could really put the hurt

On anyone who dared to cross her,
ask her to smile or subvert

So watch out shallow shitheads,
mansplainers and fools

Because Heather knows the bylaws
and she also knows the rules

But Heather's resting bytch face
was almost always used for good

And she put that scowl to work for us
like few fundraisers could

PUNK ROCK MOM + SISTER MOM JEANS

With bright blue hair and combat boots,
a nursing bra and torn jeans
Punk Rock Mom looked tough AF
but was simply PTA green

And though it seemed unlikely
that the two would ever mesh
Punk Rock Mom made fast friends
with Sister Mom Jeans/Trish

A holy roller Christian
with a knack for doing good
Trish schooled her new punk rock friend
like few insiders could

They co-chaired two committees
and ran membership as well
And when they hit that convention
they gave Sacramento hell!

The oddest couple ever
in our Parent Teacher Association
They rocked their true selves always
with shared respect and admiration

THE KINGMAKERS

Heavy is the hand that wields the gavel
thought Sister Mom Jeans as she put up her hair
Recruited to help on a Monday
by Tuesday she'd been bumped up to chair

Tasked with nominating the slate
of next year's PTA board
She found her committee mates
a little untoward

Gossip was frowned on
but ran rampant here
Alma swore like a sailor
and Kandy chugged vegan beer!

None of them took the task
as seriously as her
And the names they threw out
were beginning to blur

"We're kingmakers now,"
Mia half-joked out loud
"Just pick people we like
from the usual crowd."

Undeterred, Sister Mom Jeans
kept them on task
And everyone that they picked
agreed to be asked

So she put on some coffee
and kept them all night
And they emerged with a slate
by the dawn's early light

CHECKED OUT

As a wee kinder parent
I often wondered why
All the old fifth-grade parents
looked ready to die

They never got involved
or chaired any committees
And rarely ever rallied
around anything gritty

It's like they were just passing time
or kind of just stopped caring
And when it came to sage advice
they simply just stopped sharing

But now that I'm a fifth-grade dad
I finally understand
My fucks to give are dwindling fast
kinder parents, take command!

#VOLUNTOLD

Never
Under any circumstances
Tell your kid's teacher
What you're good at

You can't undo that shit...

TAMMY TALKS TOO LOUD

Tammy Talks Too Loud
talks too loud, even when online
Where angry, all-cap FB posts
are her go-to EVERY TIME

She's still mad they closed the Sizzler
and that Del Taco on Verdugo
And hates the traffic outside Porto's
and their Cubano con Prosciutto

A proud Magnolia Mama
from the first days of the page
Her propensity for racist rants
can really stoke some rage

Tammy longs for the good old days
when Burbank was more blonde
And you could wave away the black folks, at sundown,
with a swipe of Mickey's wand

She gets louder every year
ranting into the void
That dinosaur needs a mute button
or perhaps a new asteroid

NOBODY LOOKS PRETTY ON ZOOM
(aka MAY 2020)

We're glitchy,
we look like hell
And somewhere, off camera,
that new dad is crying

This is not how our school year
was supposed to end
But we're here
in force
online
PTA strong

Pants totally optional

WORKING MOMS

Lexie does our graphics work
Milady McRib mans our site
And Deena cuts out box tops
for us almost every night

The Nikki's run our book fair
Punk Rock Mom writes all our plays
And Dakota gardens with the kids
at lunch every Wednesday

They don't make all of our meetings
but when they do they're dressed to kill
Focused, fast and friendly
with no time to chat and chill

Chipping in on nights and weekends
after working hard all day

They help their at-home sisters
truly slay our PTA

They don't do it for the glory,
the kudos, or the pay

Most working moms just volunteer
because they know no other way

LA REINA DE LA PTA
(THE QUEEN OF THE PTA)

La Reina came from Texas
they do things bigger there

Not only folksy accents
but nails, bling and hair

She was the only daughter
in a family full of boys

And was dubbed Pequeña Reina
while still playing with her toys

She honed her regal air in high school
and all the way through college

With a knack for first-class bluffing
when it came to facts and knowledge

She was pretty and chistoso (funny)
sassy and sometimes mean

All skills which she excelled at
when she became our queen

La Reina ran our PTA

like she was holding court

A southern-fried Evita
to the presidency born!

She didn't sweat the details
or remember people's names

Or listen to detractors
while basking in acclaim

"Let them eat tapenade!" she joked
like her favorite dead French queen

At her fancy, school white party
with its breezy, Hamptons theme

I called her out once for her fakery
and was blown out like her perm

Banished from her orbit
midway through her second term

And when she moved back to Texas
where McCastles came much cheaper

La Reina and her plastic crown
vanished into la ether

PTA CONFIDENTIAL

Tim Burton went to school here
while honing his dark arts
Under our Mayberry veneer
of mid-century homes and parks

We have streets named after movie stars
and a Johnny Carson Park
And a ladies' night with food trucks
that kicks off just after dark

We have close to 50 Girl Scout troops
in a town 17.35 square miles wide
And though we don't always agree
we thrive on small town pride

We vaccinate, we vote
and shop locally too
And though most of us are transplants
we bleed dark Dodger blue

Our schools test well, best in the state
and man, our teachers rock
And that lady from that show you like
lives just down the block

I can't speak for the other schools
but our PTA game is woke
Active, involved and trade guild proud
our passion is no joke

That doesn't make us perfect
or even halfway there
So, if you wanna help us out
by all means, pull up a chair

No, not that one! That's where Pam sits!

ABOUT THE AUTHOR

Tomás Romero is an award-winning writer-producer from Los Angeles. He has written screenplays for Paramount, Sony, 20th Century Fox, Telemundo and MTV. This is his first book of poetry.

A native of Santa Cruz, CA, Romero currently lives in Burbank with his wife and tweenage daughter. He has been a card-carrying member of the Burbank PTA since 2014.

www.ingramcontent.com/pod-product-compliance
Lightning Source LLC
Chambersburg PA
CBHW071635040426
42452CB00009B/1641